Essential
Listening Skills for
College Students

Shukei Funada

Asahi Press

音声再生アプリ「リスニング・トレーナー」を使った 音声ダウンロード

朝日出版社開発のアプリ、「リスニング・トレーナー（リストレ）」を使えば、教科書の音声を
スマホ、タブレットに簡単にダウンロードできます。どうぞご活用ください。

◉ アプリ【リスニング・トレーナー】の使い方

《アプリのダウンロード》

App Store または Google Play から
「リスニング・トレーナー」のアプリ
（無料）をダウンロード

App Storeは
こちら▶

Google Playは
こちら▶

《アプリの使い方》

① アプリを開き「コンテンツを追加」をタップ
② 画面上部に【15652】を入力しDoneをタップ

音声ストリーミング配信 ≫≫

この教科書の音声は、
右記ウェブサイトにて
無料で配信しています。

https://text.asahipress.com/free/english/

はじめに

　学生時代にアメリカに留学していた時に，英語の音変化について経験したことで，未だに鮮明に記憶に残っていることが2つあります。

　1つ目は，a lot of の綴り方についてです。あるアメリカ人から「a lot of はこれまでずっと，alot of の二語だと思っていたが，今日初めて，英文法の授業で，a lot of の三語だと知った」と聞かされたことがありました。これには驚きました。アメリカ人は日本人とは違い，英語を連結した音として覚えるために，a lot of は，alot と of の二語から成り立っていると捉えていたわけです。日本人なら文字から英語を覚えるために，a lot of は3つの単語から成り立っていて，音のまとまりとして，alot と of に分けられるとは思いもつかないことでしょう。

　2つ目は，同じクラスにいたアメリカ人のメモ帳の見出しが，Things I gotta do today となっていたことです。gotta は「〜しなければならない」という意味の have got to から have が脱落して，got と to が連結したときの発音綴りです。[t] が有声化して「ガラ」のように発音されます。会話では gotta は，I gotta go. You gotta do what you gotta do. などでよく出てくるのですが，これが書かれた文字にも使われていたことに衝撃を受けました。

　この2つの体験が意味するのは，ネイティブ・スピーカーがナチュラル・スピードで話す英語では，「語と語の空きは音と音との空きではない」「綴りと音とは一致しない」ということになるでしょう。そして，このことを踏まえたうえで，英語を生の音として記憶する訓練が，スピーキングやリスニングの力をつけるためには，どうしても必要になってきます。

　本書は，アメリカ英語における音変化を，知識として知っているだけではなく，音変化によって生じる音を，自分でも再生できることを目標に書かれています。各Unit は，音変化の詳しい解説とディクテーションやリスリングの練習問題から構成されています。

　本書を手にした皆さんは，付属の音声を徹底的に活用して，音声を聞いたら瞬時に英文の意味が理解でき，同じ音を自分でも出せるまで訓練を続けてください。そして，英語を覚えるとは，「音の塊を意味とともに記憶することである」ということを実感してほしいと思います。

　最後に，本書の出版を強く勧めてくださった編集部の皆さんには，企画の段階から大変お世話になりました。ここに改めて感謝の意を表したいと思います。

船田秀佳

目 次

have got to（gotta），has got to（～'s gotta），give me（gimme），let me（lemme）における同化を学びます。括弧内の gotta, gimme,lemme は発音綴りで，発音される音をそのまま綴ったものです。

冠詞，前置詞，助動詞，be 動詞，人称代名詞には発音の際，強勢が置かれず，弱く発音されます。

接続詞，関係詞，不定形容詞，完了形で用いられる been には，発音の際，強勢が置かれず，弱く発音されます。

速い会話では，曖昧母音 [ə] のような語中の母音や [t] [d] などの子音が発音されないで脱落する現象が起きます。

語が連続するとき，先行語の末尾子音と後続語の語頭子音が，同一子音，同一調音点子音などの場合は，先行語の末尾子音が発音されないで脱落します。

語が連続するとき，先行語の末尾子音と後続語の語頭母音が連結する現象が起き，二語が一語のように発音されます。

先行語の末尾子音と後続語の語頭母音の連結を，さらに熟語の中で見ていきます。熟語としては，二語や三語から成り立っていますが，音声的には，一語のように聞こえます。

better は「ベラ」のように発音されます。これは，強母音と弱母音の間に挟まれた [t] が，有声化するために起きる現象です。たたき音と呼ばれるこの [t] の有声化について学びます。

本 書 の 使 い 方

　本書は，ネイティブ・スピーカーが，自然なスピードで話す時に生じる音変化について，頭で理解するだけではなく，口と耳を使ってトレーニングすることを主眼としています。そこで，以下の点に留意していただきたいと思います。

◆ 付属の音声について

　付属の音声を用いて次の2つの訓練をしてください。

　　1. 音変化のルールを理解し，英文を見ながら音声の後につけてリピートする。

　　2. 英文を見ないで音声の後につけてリピートできるようにする。

◆ カタカナ表記について

　英語の生の音は，カタカナでは表記できないとして，発音記号やアルファベットで音を表す方法があります。例えば，meet you を［míːtʃu］，meechu で音を表記するといったものです。

　しかし，本書はカタカナでイメージ音を記しています。これは，生の音が出せるようになる訓練の過程で，カタカナを利用することは構わないという立場を取っているからです。

　例えば，今あげた meet you は「ミーチュ」としてあります。もちろん，カタカナでは正確に表記できない with の［ð］，right の［r］，link の［l］などの音は，正確に発音できることが前提です。

◆ 発声法について

　英語と日本語の発声法については，大きな違いがあります。英語は，声帯が緩み，声道が広げられ，顎や唇を頻繁に動かして，音が出される傾向があります。これに対して，日本語は，声帯が張り詰め，声道が狭まり，顎や唇をあまり動かさないで，音が出されがちです。

　英語の音を出すときは，「脱力」がポイントです。発声器官の力を抜くことから始めましょう。冷えたビールを飲んで「あー，美味しい」という時の「あー」を，下顎を思いっきり下げて言ってみましょう。これで声道が広がります。この後，息を吸い込んで下腹にためてから，低声で発音しましょう。そうすれば，よく通る響きのある音を出すことができます。

◆ 実践が大切

　アメリカで受けた英語音声学の授業では，日本で受けたものとは大きく異なり，学期中に3分間スピーチを数回行い，その中で個々の音がきちんと出されているかどうかをチェックされました。

これは，優れたやり方だと思いました。なぜなら，スピーチとなると人前であがってしまい，教科書を見ながらなら発音できる音が，うまく出せないことがあるからです。

　3分間スピーチは，次のような項目について，それぞれ5段階で採点されました。

① オープニングセンテンス　② 内容　③ 構成　④ 語彙　⑤ 結論

⑥ 視線　⑦ 身振り手振り　⑧ 姿勢　⑨ 時間　⑩ 発音　⑪抑揚

⑫ 声の通り

さらに，改善すべき点と総評が文章で書かれたものが渡されました。

　このように，スピーチの中でちゃんと音が出せるかどうかを調べる方法は，発音を上達させるうえで，是非取り入れるべきだと思います。

　読者の皆さんは，付属の音声の後につけて発音練習するだけではなく，実際のスピーチや会話の中で，音変化に沿った音が出せるかどうかチェックしてみてください。

Unit 1 | 子音の結合

1. **Frankl**in is good at **ski**ing, **sk**ating and **sn**owboarding.
2. I bu**mped** into **Bradl**ey at the boo**kst**ore this a**ft**ernoon.
3. How was your **tr**ip to **Spr**ing**f**ield, **Kr**istie?
4. Ran**dolph dr**ives to **sch**ool **thr**ee days a week.
5. **Gl**oria is **cl**eaning the be**dr**oom on the fir**st fl**oor.
6. What **br**ought wi**despr**ead **dr**ough**ts** in Au**str**alia this summer?
7. **Alfr**ed had two **sl**ices of **br**ead and a **gl**ass of mi**lk** for **br**eak**fast**.
8. Mr. Ar**mstr**ong can **sp**eak En**gl**ish, **Sp**anish and Bu**lg**arian **fl**uent**ly**.

● 英語の音声は，母音と子音に分類でき，母音は呼気が口の中で発声器官の妨げを受けずに出される音，子音は呼気が発声器官の妨げを受けて出される音です。

● 日本語の「花」を発音すると，[ha-na] のように2つのまとまりを感じることができます。このように母音を中心にした音声的な区切りの単位が音節です。
英語の音節は日本語の音節と違って，**strength** のように母音の前後に子音を従えることがよくあります。日本語式に「ストレングス」と発音すると [sutoreŋuθu] となり，母音の [u] と [o] が入ってしまいます。日本語の音節は必ず母音で終わります。この特徴を英語の発音に持ち込んで，語末はもちろん，語中の子音の後にも母音を付けないように注意しましょう。

● 子音の連続を単語の中で見てみましょう。[C：子音（consonant），V：母音（vowel）]

① 語頭の子音の連続

1. CCV　　**br**eak **tr**end **pr**esent **fl**ower **sk**in **gl**ue
2. CCCV　**spr**ead **spl**ash **str**ategy **str**ange **scr**ap **squ**eeze
　　☆3つの子音が連続するときの音は，[spr] [spl] [str] [skr] [skw] のみです。

② 語中の子音の連続

1. VCCV　　　hea**dl**ight cu**st**om ba**sk**et o**bj**ect a**ppl**ication
2. VCCCV　　a**str**ology ca**mpf**ire i**ntr**overt chi**ldr**en mi**ndf**ul
3. VCCCCV　dou**blesp**eak co**nstr**aint i**nstr**uction u**pstr**eam

③ 語末の子音の連続

1. VCC　　　he**lp** ta**ble** ri**sk** ha**lt** sa**les** hea**lth** be**lch**
2. VCCC　　so**lved** pu**mps** di**nks** mo**nths** te**mple** fi**lms**
3. VCCCC　wri**nkles** twe**lfths** sa**mples** bu**ndles** rese**mbled**

Practice A

Drill 1 Word dictation in sentences

1. My brother is a (   ) (   ) (   ).
2. (   ) (   ) is (   ) with many (   ) every day.
3. All my family (   ) are (   ) of our (   ).
4. The boy (   ) to (   ) the pine (   ).
5. My (   ) gave me a (   ) as a (   ) (   ).

Drill2 Word dictation in dialogues

1. A: Can I walk to (   ) (   ) (   ) here?
   B: Yes, you can. It's (   ) (   ) away.
2. A: How many hours did you (   ) (   ) night?
   B: I (   ) about eight hours.
3. A: I hear you can (   ) the (   ).
   B: Yes, and I can (   ) the (   ) as well.
4. A: I'll (   ) the (   ) (   ). How about you?
   B: I'll have the (   ) (   ) and the (   ) (   ).
5. A: What is (   ) doing (   )?
   B: He's reading comic (   ).

Drill 3 Sentence dictation

1. _____

2. _____

3. _____

4. _____

5. _____

Practice B

9
Listen to the statement and choose the best response.

1. (A) (B) (C)
2. (A) (B) (C)
3. (A) (B) (C)
4. (A) (B) (C)
5. (A) (B) (C)

Practice C

10
Listen to the short conversation and answer the questions.

1. What do these two people do?
   (A) They work in an office.
   (B) They're self-employed.
   (C) They're out of work.
   (D) They're students.

2. In what field of study is the woman going to work on her degrees?
   (A) Economics
   (B) Psychology
   (C) Therapy
   (D) Politics

3. According to the man, what counts a lot in getting a job?
   (A) Professional skills related to work
   (B) Good grades
   (C) Communication skills
   (D) Determination to work

11
Practice D

Listen to the short conversation and choose the best statement to complete the conversation.

1. (A) (B) (C)
2. (A) (B) (C)
3. (A) (B) (C)

Unit 2 | 音の短縮（1）

Check Point

12

1. **I'm** twenty-three years old.
2. **He's** from San Francisco.
3. **We're** close friends.
4. **It's** hot and humid today.
5. **There's** no doubt about it.
6. **Here's** to you!
7. **That's** impossible.
8. **What's** the largest city in Canada?
9. **When's** the lunch meeting?
10. **How're** things going?
11. **I'd** like vanilla ice cream.
12. **I'd** learned Italian before I left for Rome.

●I am ⇒ I'm のように短縮形は綴りの点だけではなく，音も短縮されます。以下の短縮のルールを覚えておきましょう。

① **人称代名詞＋ be 動詞**

I am ⇒ I'm　you are ⇒ you're　we are ⇒ we're　they are ⇒ they're
he is ⇒ he's　she is ⇒ she's　it is ⇒ it's

② **疑問詞＋ be 動詞**

who is ⇒ who's　what is ⇒ what's　when is ⇒ when's
why is ⇒ why's　where is ⇒ where's　how is ⇒ how's
who are ⇒ who're　what are ⇒ what're　how are ⇒ how're

③ **指示代名詞＋ be 動詞**

that is ⇒ that's

④ **副詞＋ be 動詞**

here is ⇒ here's　there is ⇒ there's　there are ⇒ there're

⑤ **人称代名詞＋ would［had］**

I would［had］⇒ I'd　you would［had］⇒ you'd　we would［had］⇒ we'd
he would［had］⇒ he'd　she would［had］⇒ she'd　it would［had］⇒ it'd
they would［had］⇒ they'd
☆ 'd が would か had のどちらなのかは，後ろに原形動詞か過去分詞のいずれかが続くのかによります。文法力も必要です。

Practice A

13

Drill 1 Word dictation in sentences

1. (   ) Alan Gordon of ABC Company.
2. (   ) always welcome.
3. (   ) optimistic about everything.
4. (   ) three oranges on the table.
5. (   ) like to cancel my reservation.

14

Drill 2 Word dictation in dialogues

1. A: (   ) everything going with you?
   B: (   ) cool.
2. A: (   ) the nearest post office?
   B: (   ) just around the corner.
3. A: (   ) your family doing?
   B: (   ) all doing okay.
4. A: (   ) wrong? You look pale.
   B: (   ) fine. I just drank too much last night.
5. A: (   ) Ted, I believe.
   B: No, (   ) not. (   ) Jack.

15

Drill 3 Sentence dictation

1. _____

2. _____

3. _____

4. _____

5. _____

Practice B

16

Listen to the statement and choose the best response.

1. (A) (B) (C)
2. (A) (B) (C)
3. (A) (B) (C)
4. (A) (B) (C)
5. (A) (B) (C)

Practice C

17

Listen to the short conversation and answer the questions.

1. How's the man's physical condition?
   (A) Hungover
   (B) Exhausted
   (C) Stocky
   (D) Critically ill

2. About how many words can the man read in three minutes?
   (A) About 500
   (B) About 1,000
   (C) About 1,500
   (D) About 2,000

3. What did the man think about the woman's comment on his English ability?
   (A) He was criticized.
   (B) He was neglected.
   (C) He was given a pep-talk.
   (D) He was flattered.

Practice D

18

Listen to the short conversation and choose the best statement to complete the conversation.

1. (A) (B) (C)
2. (A) (B) (C)
3. (A) (B) (C)

Unit 3 | 音の短縮（2）

Check Point

19

1. **I'll** be busy next week.
2. **You'll** find the detective story interesting.
3. **She'll** go shopping with her mother tomorrow.
4. **It'll** be windy this evening.
5. **That'll** be fine with me.
6. **There'll** be a speech contest next Friday.
7. **We've** known each other for ten years.
8. **I've** got ten bucks in my pocket.
9. **He's** got three Canadian friends.
10. With more money she **would've** bought that fur coat.
11. She **could've** missed the express train.
12. I **should've** learned how to speak English.
13. Studying abroad in America **must've** been an exciting experience.
14. You **might've** heard about that story.

● I'll は I will の短縮形です。'll の ［l］の音は暗い響きがするので，dark ［l］（ダークエル）と呼ばれ，日本語のウのように聞こえてきます。

● 例文 9 の He's got は He has got の短縮形です。主語が 3 人称単数でない場合は，I have got ⇒ I've got, We have got ⇒ We've got のようになります。さらに，have が脱落して，I got, We got になることがあります。過去形ではありません。

● イメージ音

 1. I'll：アイウ 2. You'll：ユーウ 3. She'll：シーウ 4. It'll：イル

 5. That'll：ザル 6. There'll：ゼアル 7. We've：ウィヴ

 8. I've：アイヴ 9. He's：ヒズ

● 助動詞 + have +過去分詞の短縮形とイメージ音は以下の通りです。

 10. would have ⇒ would've ⇒ woulda
　　　　　　　　　　　ウダヴ　　　ウダ
 11. could have ⇒ could've ⇒ coulda
　　　　　　　　　　　クダヴ　　　クダ
 12. should have ⇒ should've ⇒ shoulda
　　　　　　　　　　　シュダヴ　　　シュダ
 13. must have ⇒ must've ⇒ musta
　　　　　　　　　　　マスタヴ　　　マスタ
 14. might have ⇒ might've ⇒ mighta
　　　　　　　　　　　マイダヴ　　　マイタ

☆ 3 列目は have が弱母音[ə]になったときの発音綴りです。英文を書くときは使いません。

Practice   A

Drill 1 Word dictation in sentences

1. (   ) come and see us this afternoon.
2. (   ) be a rock concert at Tokyo Dome next month.
3. (   ) got three million yen in her savings account.
4. (   ) lived in San Diego for twenty years.
5. He (   ) studied hard for the English exam.

Drill2 Word dictation in dialogues

1. A: How much is it all together?
   B: (   ) be 350 dollars, sir.
2. A: Do you have any idea when (   ) be back?
   B: She said (   ) be back by seven o'clock.
3. A: (   ) got a serious problem.
   B: Don't worry. (   ) help you solve it.
4. A: (   ) been three years since you came to Los Angeles.
   B: How time flies! (   ) be happy to live here for another
      ten years.
5. A: Maybe you (   ) called me beforehand.
   B: I'm sorry. (   ) lost your phone number.

Drill 3 Sentence dictation

1.

2. _____

3. _____

4. _____

5. _____

Practice B

Listen to the statement and choose the best response.

1. (A) (B) (C)
2. (A) (B) (C)
3. (A) (B) (C)
4. (A) (B) (C)
5. (A) (B) (C)

Practice C

Listen to the short conversation and answer the questions.

1. How much is the woman going to pay in total?
   (A) $ 4,500
   (B) $ 4,680
   (C) $ 5,350
   (D) $ 5,960
2. What is the form for?
   (A) A refund
   (B) A ticket
   (C) A lottery
   (D) A social security number
3. Who most likely is the man?
   (A) A visitor
   (B) A public accountant
   (C) A regular customer
   (D) A sales clerk

Practice D

Listen to the short conversation and choose the best statement to complete the conversation.

1. (A) (B) (C)
2. (A) (B) (C)
3. (A) (B) (C)

Check Point

26

1. He **isn't** worried about the results of the job interview.
2. You **aren't** old enough to drink.
3. I **wasn't** in Sacramento last week.
4. We **weren't** allowed to take picitures inside the museum.
5. I **don't** understand what you mean.
6. He **doesn't** like physics.
7. She **didn't** go to the supermarket yesterday.
8. I **haven't** been to Europe yet.
9. It's been ages, **hasn't** it?
10. I just **can't** seem to quit smoking.
11. Hurry up! You **mustn't** be late for the exam.
12. I **won't** be able to attend the meeting next Monday.
13. I **wouldn't** mind a cup of coffee.
14. You **shouldn't** drive under the influence.
15. He **couldn't** be better as a planning manager.

● be 動詞 / 助動詞 + not の短縮形とイメージ音です。[n] [t] とも舌先を上の歯茎
の後ろにつけて発音されます。n't もこの状態のまま鼻から息を抜く感じで日本語
の「ント」のように発音されるので，[t] の音はほとんど聞こえてきません。

①　be 動詞＋ not

is not ⇒ isn't：イズン　are not ⇒ aren't：アーン

was not ⇒ wasn't：ワズン　were not ⇒ weren't：ワーン

②　助動詞＋ not

★ do {does/did} + not

do not ⇒ don't：ドン　does not ⇒ doesn't：ダズン

did not ⇒ didn't：ディドゥン

★ have {has} + not

have not ⇒ haven't：ハヴン　has not ⇒ hasn't：ハズン

★ will {would/can/could/must/should} + not

will not ⇒ won't：ウォン　would not ⇒ wouldn't：ウドゥン

can not ⇒ can't：キャン　could not ⇒ couldn't：クドゥン

must ⇒ mustn't：マスン　should not ⇒ shouldn't：シュドゥン

Practice A

Drill 1 Word dictation in sentences

1. I (   ) know why he (   ) agree to our plan.
2. You (   ) cut class. It (   ) do you any good.
3. There (   ) a park in this neighborhood.
4. He said he (   ) go to the gym this weekend.
5. I (   ) know you could speak Chinese.

Drill2 Word dictation in the dialogues

1. A: The movie (   ) interesting at all, was it?
   B: I (   ) agree more.
2. A: Why (   ) we go for a drive in my car this weekend?
   B: I'm afraid I (   ) join you. I've got a lot of things to do.
3. A: Please (   ) put too much salt in the soup.
   B: All right, I (   ).
4. A: There (   ) any whiskey left in the bottle.
   B: Is that so? I (   ) aware of it.
5. A: You (   ) eat and drink so much.
   B: Maybe I (   ). I'm gaining weight.

Drill 3 Sentence dictation

1.

_____

2.

_____

3.

_____

4.

_____

5.

_____

Practice   B

Listen to the statement and choose the best response.

1. (A) (B) (C)
2. (A) (B) (C)
3. (A) (B) (C)
4. (A) (B) (C)
5. (A) (B) (C)

Practice   C

Listen to the short conversation and answer the questions.

1. Who is knowledgeable about Vietnam?
   (A) Mr. Carson
   (B) Ms. Wang
   (C) Peter
   (D) Jessica

2. How many factories do they have at present?
   (A) 3
   (B) 4
   (C) 5
   (D) 6

3. What are the man and woman not talking about?
   (A) Welcoming new colleagues
   (B) Constructing factories
   (C) Opening offices
   (D) Increasing domestic demand

Practice   D

Listen to the short conversation and choose the best statement to complete the conversation.

1. (A) (B) (C)
2. (A) (B) (C)
3. (A) (B) (C)

Unit 5 | 音の同化（1）

Check Point

1. Di**d y**ou tell your mother the news?
2. What di**d y**ou have for dinner?
3. Who di**d y**ou go shopping with?
4. How di**d y**ou like Greece?
5. Coul**d y**ou wait here a minute, please?
6. Woul**d y**ou mind turning off the air conditioner?
7. Min**d y**our step.
8. Hol**d y**our horses. He'll be here in a minute.
9. We nee**d y**our help badly.
10. Nice to mee**t y**ou, Michael.
11. What brough**t y**ou to London?
12. I'll ge**t y**ou a good lawyer.
13. Won'**t y**ou join us for dinner?
14. I'll le**t y**ou know my schedule as soon as possible.
15. I'm sorry I didn't ge**t y**our name.

● 音の同化とは, 隣り合う 2 つの音が互いに影響しあって, 調音方法に変化が起き, 両方の音に類似した別の音が作り出される現象です。例文の 1～9 は [d] と [j] が互いに影響しあって, [dʒ] に変化しています。例文の 10～15 は [t] と [j] が互いに影響しあって [tʃ] が生じています。

● イメージ音

[d] + [j] ⇒ [dʒ]

1. 2. 3. 4. Did you, did you：ディジュ　5. Could you：クジュ

6. Would you：ウジュ　7. Mind your：マインジュア

8. Hold your：ホウジュア

9. need your：ニージュア

[t] + [j] ⇒ [tʃ]

10. meet you：ミーチュ　11. brought you：ブローチュ

12. get you：ゲチュ　13. Won't you：ウォンチュ　14. let you：レチュ

15. get your：ゲチュア

Practice　A

Drill 1　Word dictation in sentences

1.　I'll (　　　　) (　　　　　　) through to the Finance Section.
2.　I (　　　　) (　　　　　) not to call me after eleven o'clock.
3.　How (　　　) (　　　) (　　　) (　　　　) first month's pay?
4.　Don't worry.　He'll (　　　　) (　　　) (　　　) (　　　) need.
5.　How (　　　　) (　　　) say such a thing?

Drill2　Word dictation in dialogues

1.　A: When (　　　　) (　　　　　) go to Denmark?
　　B: We went there (　　　　) (　　　　).
2.　A: How (　　　　) (　　　　) like your steak done?
　　B: Rare, please.
3.　A: (　　　　) (　　　　) break this hundred-dollar bill?
　　B: Certainly.　(　　　　) (　　　　) like twenties?
4.　A: What (　　) (　　) (　　) (　　　) husband for his birthday?
　　B: I got him a cool tie.
5.　A: You're studying English very hard, (　　　　) (　　　　)?
　　B: Yes, I am.　How (　　　　) (　　　　)?

Drill 3　Sentence dictation

1.

2. _____

3. _____

4. _____

5. _____

Practice B
37

Listen to the statement and choose the best response.

1. (A) (B) (C)
2. (A) (B) (C)
3. (A) (B) (C)
4. (A) (B) (C)
5. (A) (B) (C)

Practice C
38

Listen to the short talk and answer the questions.

1. How can the result of the exam be described?
   (A) Super
   (B) Terrible
   (C) Pretty good
   (D) Satisfactory

2. Who is bad at math?
   (A) Monica
   (B) Michelle
   (C) Alex
   (D) Mark

3. Why didn't the man ask his sister for help?
   (A) She is poor at statistics.
   (B) She got a bad grade in math last semester.
   (C) She hates geometry.
   (D) She was out of town.

Practice D
39

Listen to the short conversation and choose the best statement to complete the conversation.

1. (A) (B) (C)
2. (A) (B) (C)
3. (A) (B) (C)

Check Point

40

1. **Can y**ou recommend a good restaurant around here?
2. How ca**n y**ou be so sure?
3. May I u**se y**our dictionary?
4. When**'s y**our father coming back to Japan?
5. He nee**ds y**our candid opinion.
6. What make**s y**ou think so?
7. I'll fi**x y**our bicycle this afternoon.
8. **It's y**our turn to do the dishes, Albert.
9. Wha**t's y**our favorite food?
10. Can I hel**p y**ou?
11. Ha**ve y**ou ever visited Alaska?
12. What's wrong wi**th y**our PC?
13. Shall I ta**ke y**ou to our office in Shinjuku?
14. Can I as**k y**our brother to help me with my term paper?
15. I'll ma**ke y**ou a cup of jasmine tea.

● さまざまな音の同化とそのイメージ音を見てみましょう。[*n*j] の [*n*] のように，[j] の音色を帯びる音はイタリック体で示してあります。2つの単語を一語のように発音できるようにしましょう。

[n] + [j] ⇒ [*n*j]　1. 2.　Can you, can you：キャニュ

[z] + [j] ⇒ [dʒ]　3.　use your：ユージュア　4.　When's your：ウェンジュア

[dz] + [j] ⇒ [dʒ]　5.　needs your：ニージュア

[s] + [j] ⇒ [ʃ]　6.　makes you：メイクシュ　7.　fix your：フィクシュア

[ts] + [j] ⇒ [tʃ]　8.　It's your：イチュア　9.　What's your：ワチュア

[p] + [j] ⇒ [*p*j]　10.　help you：ヘルピュ

[v] + [j] ⇒ [*v*j]　11.　Have you：ハヴュ

[ð] + [j] ⇒ [*ð*j]　12.　with your：ウィジュア

[k] + [j] ⇒ [*k*j]　13.　take you：テイキュ　14.　ask your：アスキュア

15.　make you：メイキュ

Practice   A

Drill 1   Word dictation in sentences

1. I (   ) (   ) sister will study in America (   ) (   ).
2. He (   ) (   ) to lend him three hundred dollars, didn't he?
3. My GPA is about the same (   ) (   ).
4. We'll (   ) (   ) up and (   ) (   ) a movie star.
5. What (   ) (   ) so long?

Drill2   Word dictation in dialogues

1. A: (   ) (   ) room key, sir.
    B: (   ) (   ) very much.
2. A: Can I (   ) (   ) a question?
    B: Sure. What is it?
3. A: I'll (   ) (   ).
    B: I'll (   ) (   ), too.
4. A: You have to do (   ) (   ) told.
    B: All right. I'll do exactly (   ) (   ) told me.
5. A: (   ) (   ) answer the door?
    B: No problem. I'll get it.

Drill 3   Sentence dictation

1.

_____

2.

_____

3.

_____

4.

_____

5.

_____

Practice   B

Listen to the statement and choose the best response.

1. (A) (B) (C)
2. (A) (B) (C)
3. (A) (B) (C)
4. (A) (B) (C)
5. (A) (B) (C)

Practice   C

Listen to the short talk and answer the questions.

1. How much extra is the man going to pay?
    (A) $ 3
    (B) $ 4
    (C) $ 6
    (D) $ 7

2. Who is the woman?
    (A) A shop clerk
    (B) A cosmetician
    (C) A manager of the hotel
    (D) A sales manager

3. What are the daughters going to receive?
    (A) Toys
    (B) Clothing
    (C) Jewelry
    (D) Shoes

Practice   D

Listen to the short conversation and choose the best statement to complete the conversation.

1. (A) (B) (C)
2. (A) (B) (C)
3. (A) (B) (C)

Unit 7 | 音 の 同 化 （3）

Check Point

1. I **want to** [**wanna**] be a vet in the future.
2. I **want to** [**wanna**] get a license to teach English.
3. Where do you **want to** [**wanna**] go during the winter vacation?
4. I'm **going to** [**gonna**] study abroad in Germany next year.
5. I'm **going to** [**gonna**] go surfing this weekend.
6. Are you **going to** [**gonna**] move to Houston?
7. You **have to** contact him as soon as possible.
8. The work **has to** be finished by next Monday.
9. I **had to** do it all by myself.
10. We **had to** take shelter till the rain stopped.

- want to の発音綴りは，wanna です。want の [t] と to の [t] と [t] が連続しているために，want の [t] が脱落して [wɑntə] になります。さらに，[t] は鼻音の [n] の影響を受けて鼻音化するために [wɑnə] に変化します。発音は日本語の「ワナ」「ウォナ」の感じです。また，want a の発音綴りも wanna で，Wanna ride?（Want a ride?）I wanna cold beer.（I want a cold beer.）のようになります。

- going to の発音綴りは gonna です。going は ng の音 [ŋ] の後半部分が消えて [n] になり [gouin] になります。to の [t] は，鼻音の [n] の影響を受けて鼻音化して [nə] となり [gouinə] に変化します。そこから，母音の [i] が消え，[ou] が弱母音化して [gənə] となります。発音は日本語の「ガナ」「ゴナ」の感じです。I'm gonna は，5 のように「アイムナ」と発音されることもあります。

- 英文を書くときは，want to, going to と書きましょう。

- have to は，have の [v] が [t] の影響を受けて [f] になり to と連結するために「ハフタ」のような音になります。

- has to は，has の [z] が [t] の影響を受けて [s] になり to と連結するために「ハスタ」のような音になります。

- had to は，had の [d] と to の [t] が同一調音点の子音で連続しているために [d] が脱落して to と連結して「ハットゥ」のような音になります。

Practice A

48

Drill 1 Word dictation in sentences

1. Is he (　　　　) (　　　　　　) make a speech in English tomorrow?
2. We (　　　　) (　　　　　　) know the truth first and foremost.
3. He (　　　　) (　　　　　) eat less meat to lose weight.
4. How are you (　　　　) (　　　　) spend your summer vacation?
5. I (　　　　) (　　　　) go to the dentist today.

49

Drill 2 Word dictation in dialogues

1. A: When are you (　　　　) (　　　　　) leave for the UK?
   I (　　　) (　　　　) see you off at the airport.
   B: Two weeks from today. You don't (　　　) (　　　) if you're busy.
2. A: What are you (　　　　) (　　　　) do on Friday?
   B: I'm (　　　) (　　　　) go cycling with my friends.
3. A: Are you (　　　) (　　　　) stay up late this week?
   B: Yes. I (　　　) (　　　　) finish my research paper by
   Saturday morning.
4. A: What do you (　　　) (　　　　) drink?
   B: I (　　　) (　　　　) drink some red wine. How about you?
5. A: What advice do you (　　　) (　　　　) give to him?
   B: He (　　　) (　　　) study statistics.

50

Drill 3 Sentence Dictation

1. _____

2. _____

3. _____

4. _____

5. _____

Practice B

51

Listen to the statement and choose the best response.

1. (A) (B) (C)
2. (A) (B) (C)
3. (A) (B) (C)
4. (A) (B) (C)
5. (A) (B) (C)

Practice C

52

Listen to the short talk and answer the questions.

1. How did the man feel about the woman's explanation?
   (A) Relieved
   (B) Saddened
   (C) Shocked
   (D) Disappointed

2. Who are the speakers?
   (A) An academic advisor and a student
   (B) A mother and her son
   (C) A professor and his student
   (D) A consultant and his client

3. What did the woman major in at college?
   (A) Music
   (B) Geology
   (C) Chinese
   (D) Sociology

Practice D

53

Listen to the short conversation and choose the best statement to complete the conversation.

1. (A) (B) (C)
2. (A) (B) (C)
3. (A) (B) (C)

Unit 8 | 音の同化（4）

Check Point

1. **I've got to** [**I gotta**] bring my cholesterol down.
2. **I've got to** [**I gotta**] get up at 4:30 tomorrow morning.
3. **You've got to** [**You gotta**] help me find a good job.
4. **We've got to** [**We gotta**] do what **we've got to** [**we gotta**] do.
5. **Give me** [**Gimme**] a break.
6. **Give me** [**Gimme**] another chance to do it.
7. **Give me** [**Gimme**] a clue about who he is.
8. **Let me** [**Lemme**] think about it.
9. **Let me** [**Lemme**] give it a try.
10. **Let me** [**Lemme**] talk to Katherine.

- 「～しなければならない」という意味の have got to は，会話では have が脱落して got to となります。次に got の［t］が脱落して［gɑtə］となります。さらに，［t］は強い強勢のある母音と弱い強勢のある母音に挟まれているので有声化して，日本語の「ラ」に近い音になります。これを発音綴りで表すと gotta になり，日本語の「ガラ」で置き換えることができます。（［t］の有声化については Unit15 で詳しく扱います）gotta はくだけた言い方で「～しなきゃ」という意味を表します。

- has got to の場合は，has は脱落しませんから，He's gotta go to work today. のようになります。

- give me の発音綴りは gimme です。give の［v］が［m］の影響を受けて無声音になり，さらに［m］に同化するために起きる現象です。gimme は「ギミ」と発音して構いません。

- let me の発綴りは lemme です。let の［t］が［m］の影響を受けて無声音になり，さらに［m］に同化するために起きる現象です。lemme の発音はカタカナでは「レミ」となります。ただし，「レ」は日本語で代用するのではなく，［l］を正確に発音しましょう。

- 英文を書くときは，I've got to, give me, let me と書きましょう。

Practice A

Drill 1 Word dictation in sentences

1. (　　　　　) (　　　　　) (　　　　　) remember.
   (　　　　　) (　　　　　) (　　　　　) get to the airport by 8:30 A.M.
2. (　　　　　) (　　　　　) know the answer to the question.
3. (　　　　　) (　　　　　) (　　　　　) repeat English 250 next semester.
4. Could you (　　　　　) (　　　　　) your email address?
5. (　　　　　) (　　　　　) (　　　　　) give her more details.

Drill2 Word dictation in dialogues

1. A: Would you please (　　　　　) (　　　　　) a fork?
   B: Sure. Here you are.
2. A: (　　　　　) (　　　　　) (　　　　　) go now.
   B: Can't you stay a little longer?
3. A: What can I do for you?
   B: (　　　　　) (　　　　　) your candid opinion about our project.
4. A: (　　　　　) (　　　　　) (　　　　　) finish up our work by the
      end of this month.
   B: You're right. (　　　　　) (　　　　　) (　　　　　) give it all we've got.
5. A: (　　　　　) (　　　　　) tell you something.
   B: Go ahead. What is it?

Drill 3 Sentence dictation

1.

2.

3.

4.

5.

58

Practice   B

Listen to the statement and choose the best response.

1. (A) (B) (C)
2. (A) (B) (C)
3. (A) (B) (C)
4. (A) (B) (C)
5. (A) (B) (C)

59

Practice   C

Listen to the short talk and answer the questions.

1. Where will the man be next month?
   (A) In Europe
   (B) In Asia
   (C) In North America
   (D) In Latin America

2. What's bugging the man?
   (A) They have a shortage of manpower.
   (B) They're getting lower profits in Asia.
   (C) They're out of funds.
   (D) They cannot expand the market in Europe.

3. What doesn't the woman have to let the man know?
   (A) Effective ways of publicizing their commodities
   (B) What customers want now
   (C) How to appeal to purchasers
   (D) How to cut down on expenditures

60

Practice   D

Listen to the short conversation and choose the best statement to complete the conversation.

1. (A) (B) (C)
2. (A) (B) (C)
3. (A) (B) (C)

Unit 9 | 音の弱化（1）

Check Point

1. Tim **is a** junior **at** Brown University. **Am I** right?
2. **We are** members **of the** tennis club.
3. **It was** cloudy **in** Sydney yesterday.
4. **Are you** sure **they were** here ten minutes ago?
5. Congratulations **on your** promotion **to** section chief.
6. **You can** trust Sally. **She** always keeps **her** word.
7. **Do you** know **his** name?
8. Nothing **will** make **her** change **her** mind.
9. Don't forget **to** bring **him to the** party.
10. Email **him** right away.
11. Lisa asked **him to** take **her** skiing.
12. Joyce asked **them to** leave **her** alone.
13. Let's give **them a** big hand.

● 文の中で，名詞や動詞など意味を伝えるうえで欠くことのできない内容語に対して，文法的な機能を示す機能語は比較的重みが低く強勢を受けません。その中で，このUnit では，冠詞，前置詞，助動詞，be 動詞，人称代名詞の弱化を見てみましょう。

● イメージ音

5. on your：オニャ（[juəɹ] の弱形で [jəɹ]）
6. You can：ユークン（can [kæn] の弱形で [kən]/[kn]）
   keeps her：キープサ（[h] の脱落）
7. Do you：ドゥー his name：イズネイム（[h] の脱落）
8. make her：メイカー（[h] の脱落） change her：チェンジア（[h] の脱落）
9. bring him：ブリンギム（[h] の脱落）
10. email him：イーメイリム（[h] の脱落）
11. asked him：アスティム take her：テイカー（[h] の脱落）（asked の発音は [æst]）
12. asked them：アステム（[ð] の脱落） leave her：リーヴァ（[h] の脱落）
13. give them：ギヴェム（[ð] の脱落）

● 通常前置詞は強勢を受けませんが，文末の前置詞は次のようにやや強く発音されます。

1. I have no idea what he is driving **at**?   2. Who are you talking **to**?
3. What is he looking **for**?   4. Where are you **from**?

Practice A

Drill 1 Word Dictation in sentences

62

1. (   ) (   ) have (   ) email address?

2. (   ) took (   ) daughter (   ) (   )
    amusement park (   ) Saturday.

3. I am Richard. Call (   ) Rich (   ) short.

4. First period begins (   ) 9:10 (   ) (   ) school.

5. (   ) gave (   ) (   ) cellphone number.

Drill2 Word Dictation in dialogues

63

1. A: (   ) (   ) like apple pies?

    B: Apple pies? I love (   )!

2. A: (   ) miss (   ) a lot.

    B: So do I. (   ) want (   ) to come back right away.

3. A: When did (   ) visit (   ) uncle (   ) Brisbane?

    B: (   ) believe (   ) (   ) two weeks ago.

4. A: (   ) (   ) met (   ) before?

    B: Yes, I have. (   ) met (   ) three years ago (   ) Tokyo.

5. A: Please tell (   ) (   ) call (   ) (   ) evening.

    B: No problem. (   ) (   ) tell (   ) (   ) do so.

Drill 3 Sentence Dictation

64

1.

    _____

2.

    _____

3.

    _____

4.

    _____

5.

    _____

Practice   B
65

Listen to the statement and choose the best response.

1. (A) (B) (C)
2. (A) (B) (C)
3. (A) (B) (C)
4. (A) (B) (C)
5. (A) (B) (C)

Practice   C
66

Listen to the short talk and answer the questions.

1. How many sisters does the speaker have?
   (A) 2
   (B) 3
   (C) 4
   (D) 5

2. Where was the speaker's sister when she was a second-year student at college?
   (A) Germany
   (B) Japan
   (C) Spain
   (D) Vietnam

3. What is the speaker referring to?
   (A) Language schools
   (B) Tour conductors
   (C) Globalization
   (D) Her relative

Practice   D
67

Listen to the short conversation and choose the best statement to complete the conversation.

1. (A)   (B)   (C)
2. (A)   (B)   (C)
3. (A)   (B)   (C)

Unit 10 | 音の弱化（2）

2-1

1. It's nice **and** warm today, isn't it?
2. Ladies **and** gentlemen, I give you Mr. **and** Mrs. Collins.
3. We'll go there by bus **or** by taxi.
4. We respect him **because** [**'cause**] he's diligent.
5. They canceled the hike **because** [**'cause**] it was raining heavily.
6. He looks young, **but** he is well over sixty.
7. We'd like to start our own business, **but** we lack the funds.
8. I hope **that** you get an A in English.
9. **As soon as** he finished the document, he went to the Internet café.
10. Erica is the only student **who** can speak Danish.
11. Who is the man **that** is talking with your mother?
12. This is the park **where** I met her.
13. Would you like **some** coffee?
14. Is there **any** butter left? If not, I'll go get **some**.
15. It's **been** a while. How have you **been**?

● この Unit では機能語として，接続詞，関係詞，不定形容詞に，完了形で使われる
been を取りあげます。

● イメージ音

1. nice and warm：ナイスンウォーム（[ænd] の弱形は [n]）
2. Ladies and gentlemen：レディズンジェヌルメン
   Mr. and Mrs. Colllins：ミスターンミセズコリンズ
3. bus or：バソ
4.5. 'cause：カズ
6. but he：バヒ　（[t] の脱落）　7. but we：バウィ（[t] の脱落）
8. that：ズ
9. As soon as：ァスーナズ　10. who：フ
11. that is：ザリズ（[t] の有声化）　12. where：ウェァ
13.14. some：スム（[sʌ́m] の弱形は [s(ə)m]）
14. any：エニ
15. been：ベン（[bíːn] の弱形は [bin] / [bən]）

28

Practice A

2-2

Drill 1 Word dictation in sentences

1. This is (   ) I make delicious pumpkin pies.
2. We all know (   ) you can solve these problems.
3. What a nice cup (   ) saucer!
4. I took a taxi (   ) my car broke down.
5. Do you have (   ) other questions?

2-3

Drill2 Word dictation in dialogues

1. A: Where have you (   )?
   B: I've (   ) at the beauty parlor.
2. A: Do you need (   ) salt (   ) pepper?
   B: I'm fine. Thank you.
3. A: It looks (   ) (   ) it's going to rain.
   B: You're right. Let's hurry home.
4. A: How come you can't come to the party on Saturday?
   B: (   ) I have to study for the English test.
5. A: How long have you (   ) teaching English, Paul?
   B: For twenty years. It's (   ) my (   )
      (   ) (   ).

2-4

Drill 3 Sentence Dictation

1. _____

2. _____

3. _____

4. _____

5. _____

Practice B

2-5

Listen to the statement and choose the best response.

1. (A) (B) (C)
2. (A) (B) (C)
3. (A) (B) (C)
4. (A) (B) (C)
5. (A) (B) (C)

Practice C

2-6

Listen to the short talk and answer the questions.

1. What's the woman's destination?

 (A) Singapore

 (B) Australia

 (C) Canada

 (D) USA

2. What was the woman's original flight number?

 (A) 007

 (B) 009

 (C) 115

 (D) 148

3. What does the woman want?

 (A) A morning flight

 (B) An evening flight

 (C) A long distance flight

 (D) A nonstop flight

Practice D

2-7

Listen to the short conversation and choose the best statement to complete the conversation.

1. (A) (B) (C)
2. (A) (B) (C)
3. (A) (B) (C)

Unit 11 | 音の脱落 (1)

Check Point

2-8

1. My **fam(i)ly** consists of eight people.
2. I bought this digital **cam(e)ra** yesterday.
3. She goes to **in(t)ernational** school in **T(o)ron(t)o**.
4. I have **plen(t)y** of homework to do.
5. They sell **mos(t)ly** sporting goods at that store.
6. Thank you so much for your **kin(d)ness**.
7. Larry is tall and **han(d)some**. He's **frien(d)ly** to us all.
8. The Democratic Party won a **lan(d)sli(de)** victory in the election.
9. How's it **goin(g)**?
10. Good **jo(b)**! Keep it **u(p)**!
11. Look **ou(t)**! The dump truck is **comin(g)**.
12. Is it **rainin(g)** **outsi(de)**?
13. I'll give you a **hin(t)**.
14. When will he be **ba(ck)**?
15. She was extremely tired and slept like a **lo(g)**.

● 語中や語末の音が速い会話になると，発音されないで消えてなくなることがあります。これは「音の脱落」と呼ばれています。例文で脱落の起きる音環境を見てみましょう。

例文 1，2 では family, camera の弱母音の [ə] が脱落します。この音は曖昧母音と呼ばれているもので，母音の中では最も脱落しやすい音です。

例文 3，4，5 では international, Toronto, plenty, mostly の [t] が脱落します。子音が連続したときによく脱落する音です。Toronto は，弱母音の [ə] も脱落します。

例文 6，7，8 では kindness, handsome, friendly, landslide の [d] が脱落します。landslide は語末の [d] も脱落します。

例文 9，11，12 では going, coming, raining, の ng の音 [ŋ] の後半部分が脱落して [n] になってしまう現象です。映画のシナリオなどでは，goin', comin', rain' と書かれることがあります。

例文 10〜15 では job の [b], up の [p], out, hint の [t], outside の [d], back の [k], log の [g] が脱落します。これは破裂音が文末に来るときは脱落してしまう現象です。破裂音とは，[p] [b] [t] [d] [k] [g] の6つの音を指します。発音する口の形で呼気を止めた状態を保ちましょう。息漏れはしません。

Practice A

Drill 1 Word dictation in sentences

1. She (   ) showed us the way to the station.
2. You got an F in Physics 250? That's too (   ).
3. I'd like to talk to the (   ).
4. Where can I find the nearest (   )?
5. Watch (   )! There's a puddle.

Drill2 Word dictation in dialogues

1. A: Where did you get that gorgeous (   )?
   B: At the shopping (   ) downtown.
2. A: I've made you a new blouse, (   ).
   B: Bless your (   )!
3. A: What's he (   )?
   B: He's (   ) TV in the (   ) room.
4. A: How old is your daughter?
   B: She'll be (   ) years old next month.
5. A: Do you like sociology?
   B: (   ), I hate it.

Drill 3 Sentence dictation

1.

2.

3.

4.

5.

2-12

Practice B

Listen to the statement and choose the best response.

1. (A) (B) (C)
2. (A) (B) (C)
3. (A) (B) (C)
4. (A) (B) (C)
5. (A) (B) (C)

2-13

Practice C

Listen to the short talk and answer the questions.

1. How many hats is Dr. Porter wearing?

   (A) 1

   (B) 2

   (C) 3

   (D) 4

2. How long is the seminar?

   (A) 6 hours

   (B) 7 hours

   (C) 8 hours

   (D) 9 hours

3. What's the best way to get information on the seminars?

   (A) By reading the brochure

   (B) By visiting the website

   (C) By calling Wellbeing Company

   (D) By calling Dr. Porter

2-14

Practice D

Listen to the short conversation and choose the best statement to complete the conversation.

1. (A) (B) (C)
2. (A) (B) (C)
3. (A) (B) (C)

Unit **12** 音の脱落（2）

1. Would you care for s**om**e **m**ore brandy? ［m］+［m］
2. Ta**ke c**are of yourself. ［k］+［k］
3. I fee**l l**ike **c**lam chowder and roas**t t**urkey. ［l］+［l］, ［k］+［k］, ［t］+［t］
4. Mr. Di**ck C**arter will go ro**ck c**limbing thi**s s**ummer.
   ［k］+［k］, ［k］+［k］, ［s］+［s］
5. I**s S**andra a goo**d d**ancer or a ba**d d**ancer?
   ［z］+［s］, ［d］+［d］, ［d］+［d］
6. Me**g g**ot transferre**d t**o Alice **S**prings last **m**onth.
   ［g］+［g］, ［t］+［t］, ［d］+［t］, ［s］+［s］, ［t］+［m］
7. **It** takes about **t**en minutes to ge**t t**o the next **s**top.
   ［t］+［t］, ［t］+［t］, ［t］ +［t］, ［t］+［s］
8. You mus**t b**e hungry. ［t］+［b］
9. You shoul**d t**ake the subway. ［d］+［t］

● 語末が子音の語と語頭が子音の語が連続するとき，前者の語末の子音が脱落する現象が起きます。例文1〜7の同一子音の連続，例文5の［z］+［s］，例文6，9の［d］+［t］の同一調音点子音の連続，例文6の［t］+［m］，例文7の［t］+［s］，例文8の［t］+［b］の異なる子音の連続において，先行する語の末尾の子音が脱落します。

● イメージ音

1. some more：スモア 　2. 　Take care：テイケア
3. feel like clam：フィーライクラム 　roast turkey：ロウスターキィ
4. Dick Carter：ディッカーター 　rock climbing：ロックライミン
   this summer：ジィサマー
5. Is Sandra：イサンドラ 　good dancer：グッダンサー 　bad dancer：バッダンサー
6. Meg got transferred to：メッゴットランスファートゥ
   Alice Springs：アリスプリングズ 　last month：ラスマンス
7. It takes イッテイクス 　about ten アバウテン 　get to ゲットゥ
   next stop：ネクストップ
8. must be：マスビ 　9. 　should take：シュッテイク

Practice A

2-16

Drill 1   Word dictation in sentences

1. There (   ) (   ) a (   ) (   )
    (   ) (   ) the (   ) (   ).

2. My brother, who is a (   ) (   ), is getting married
    (   ) (   ).

3. Would you like (   ) (   ) (   ) (   )?

4. The (   ) (   ) (   ) (   ) done in a minute.

5. (   ) (   ) (   ) Theory 200 (   ) (   ).

2-17

Drill2   Word dictation in dialogues

1. A: What are you studying at the University (   ) (   )?
    B: (   ) (   ) in (   ) (   ).

2. A: Please (   ) (   ). Would you like a (   ) (   )?
    B: Yes, please. I'd like (   ) (   ).

3. A: (   ) (   ) do you have?
    B: It's (   ) (   ) ten.

4. A: How's business?
    B: It (   ) (   ) better.

5. A: Would you mind cutting the (   ) (   ) (   )
    (   ) (   ) (   )?
    B: Sure. I'll be (   ) (   ).

2-18

Drill 3   Sentence Dictation

1.

2.

3.

4.

5.

Practice   B

2-19

Listen to the statement and choose the best response.

1. (A) (B) (C)
2. (A) (B) (C)
3. (A) (B) (C)
4. (A) (B) (C)
5. (A) (B) (C)

Practice   C

2-20

Listen to the short talk and answer the questions.

1. How many languages is the applicant required to speak?
    (A) 2
    (B) 3
    (C) 4
    (D) 5

2. What is the first qualification about?
    (A) Age
    (B) Income
    (C) Degree
    (D) Recommendation

3. What is the woman doing at present?
    (A) Learning a foreign language
    (B) Hunting a job
    (C) Staring her own business
    (D) Taking a mock examination

Practice   D

2-21

Listen to the short conversation and choose the best statement to complete the conversation.

1. (A)   (B)   (C)
2. (A)   (B)   (C)
3. (A)   (B)   (C)

Unit 13 | 音の連結（1）

Check Point

1. I'm afraid Mike is in bed with a bad cold.
   [m]＋母音，[k]＋母音，[z]＋母音，[ð]＋母音

2. That's a good idea. [ts]＋母音，[d]＋母音

3. You need a vacation before you become a workaholic.
   [d]＋母音，[m]＋母音

4. Let's take a break in ten minutes. [k]＋母音，[k]＋母音

5. Can I have a coffee? [n]＋母音，[v]＋母音

6. How can I get to the subway station? [n]＋母音

7. What can I do for you? [n]＋母音

8. I'm planning to stay in New York for a week. [r]＋母音

9. A number of my friends can speak Chinese. [r]＋母音

10. Diana likes Japanese food such as sushi and tempura. [tʃ]＋母音

11. I've never heard of such a story. [d]＋母音，[tʃ]＋母音

12. He'll be back in an hour. [k]＋母音，[n]＋母音，[n]＋母音

13. She has a crush on Jack. [z]＋母音，[ʃ]＋母音

14. Hold on a minute, please. [d]＋母音，[n]＋母音

15. She speaks English as if she were an American. [z]＋母音，[n]＋母音

● 語が連続するとき，先行する語の末尾音と後続する語の語頭音が連結する現象が起きます。これは音の連結と呼ばれています。これが生じる基本的な音環境は，「子音＋母音」の連続です。例文から分かるように，先行する語の末尾の子音と後続する語の語頭の母音が連結して、二語が一語のように発音されます。

● イメージ音

1. I'm afraid：アイマフレイド　Mike is in：マイキィズィン　with a：ウィザ

2. That's a：ザッツァ　good idea：グダイディア / グライディア

3. need a：ニーダ / ニーラ　become a：ビカマ

4. take a：テイカ　break in：ブレイキン　5. Can I：ケナイ　have a：ハヴァ

6. can I：ケナイ　7. What can I：ワッケナイ（What の[t]の脱落）

8. for a：フォラ　9. a number of：ァナンバロヴ　10. such as：サッチャズ

11. heard of：ハードヴ　such a：サッチャ　12. back in an hour：バッキンナンナワー

13. has a：ハザァ　crush on：クラッション　14. Hold on a：ホウルドナ

15. as if：ァズイフ　an American：ァナメリカン

37

Practice A

Drill 1 Word dictation in sentences

2-23

1. (   ) (   ) have your (   ) (   ), please?

2. We (   ) (   ) (   ) (   ) (   )
time in Hawaii this summer.

3. (   ) (   ) (   ) (   ) proposal at the meeting?

4. Tokyo is (   ) (   ) the safest cities in the world.

5. Linda (   ) (   ) shower (   ) (   ) day.

Drill2 Word dictation in dialogues

2-24

1. A: (   ) (   ) nice day.

   B: Thanks. You, too.

2. A: How about going camping next weekend?

   B: Sorry. I'll be busy. (   ) (   ) (   )
   (   ) rain (   ) (   ) (   )?

3. A: I'm (   ) (   ) what she (   ) (   ) true.

   B: I'm not sure.

4. A: Where (   ) (   ) find the men's clothing section?

   B: (   ) (   ) the third floor.

5. A: (   ) (   ) ask you a favor?

   B: Certainly. What (   ) (   ) do for you?

Drill 3 Sentence dictation

2-25

1.

   _____

2.

   _____

3.

   _____

4.

   _____

5.

   _____

2-26

Practice B

Listen to the statement and choose the best response.

1. (A) (B) (C)
2. (A) (B) (C)
3. (A) (B) (C)
4. (A) (B) (C)
5. (A) (B) (C)

2-27

Practice C

Listen to the short talk and answer the questions.

1. When is the conversation taking place?

    (A) January

    (B) February

    (C) March

    (D) April

2. Who will get a degree?

    (A) Nelly

    (B) Carol

    (C) Kathy

    (D) Ed

3. How many people are going to be at the party?

    (A) 4

    (B) 5

    (C) 6

    (D) 7

2-28

Practice D

Listen to the short conversation and choose the best statement to complete the conversation.

1. (A) (B) (C)
2. (A) (B) (C)
3. (A) (B) (C)

Unit 14 | 音の連結（2）

1.　What kin**d of** music do you listen to?　[d] ＋母音
2.　She ate a pie**ce of** cake.　[s] ＋母音
3.　May I have a cu**p of** coffee?　[p] ＋母音
4.　I've got a bun**ch of** questions to ask you.　[tʃ] ＋母音
5.　Will you fi**ll ou**t this form, please?　[l] ＋母音
6.　Joe call**ed in** sick today.　[d] ＋母音
7.　The light wen**t ou**t. It must be a power failure.　[t] ＋母音
8.　Erica turn**ed a**round and smil**ed at** me.　[d] ＋母音 , [d] ＋母音
9.　He ga**ve up o**n studying Latin two years ago.　[v] ＋母音 , [p] ＋母音
10.　Thin**k a**bout what he told you.　[k] ＋母音
11.　The train bound for Riverside is pulli**ng in** shortly.　[ŋ] ＋母音
12.　Do you belie**ve in** UFOs?　[v] ＋母音
13.　I ca**me a**cross your mother at the drugstore yesterday.　[m] ＋母音
14.　She recently too**k up** golf.　[k] ＋母音
15.　You should wor**k o**n your graduation thesis right now.　[k] ＋母音

● 「子音＋母音」の連続を，熟語の中で見てみましょう。重要なことは，語と語の空きは，音と音との空きではないということです。例えば，a piece of を見ると，語と語の空きが２つあるために，そこで音が切れて三語がバラバラに発音されるように思ってしまいます。しかし，実際の音は一語の単語のように聞こえてきます。

● イメージ音

1.　What kind of：ワッカイナ（What の [t], kind の [d], of の [v] の脱落）
2.　a piece of：ァピーサ（of の[v]の脱落）
3.　a cup of：ァカッパ（of の[v]の脱落）
4.　a bunch of：ァバンチャ（of の[v]の脱落）
5.　fill out：フィラウ（out の[t]の段落）　6.　called in：コールディン
7.　went out：ウエンタウ（out の[t]の脱落）
8.　turned around：ターンダラウンド　smiled at：スマイルダット
9.　gave up on：ゲイヴァポン
10.　Think about：シンカバウ（about の[t]の段落）　　11.　pulling in：プリンギン
12.　believe in：ビリーヴィン　13.　came across：ケイマクロス
14.　took up：トゥカップ　15.　work on：ワーコン

Practice A

Drill 1   Word Dictation in sentences

2-30

1. She was (   ) (   ) for the cocktail party.
2. You look (   ) (   ) pale. What's wrong?
3. We (   ) (   ) the airport late (   )
   (   ) the weather.
4. She (   ) (   ) all the lights before she went to bed.
5. I've (   ) (   ) that his proposal is better than mine.

Drill2   Word Dictation in the dialogue

2-31

1. A: What (   ) (   ) movies do you like?
   B: I'm (   ) (   ) comedies and action movies.
2. A: May I (   ) (   )?
   B: Sure. (   ) (   ) (   ) and have a seat.
3. A: Feel free to (   ) (   ) (   ) us.
   B: Thank you very much.
4. A: Can you (   ) (   ) my tropical fish while I'm in Las Vegas?
   B: Certainly. I'll be happy to.
5. A: How come you read so many books and magazines?
   B: Just to (   ) (   ) with the times.

Drill 3   Sentence Dictation

2-32

1.
   _____

2.
   _____

3.
   _____

4.
   _____

5.
   _____

Practice B

Listen to the statement and choose the best response.

1. (A) (B) (C)
2. (A) (B) (C)
3. (A) (B) (C)
4. (A) (B) (C)
5. (A) (B) (C)

Practice C

Listen to the short talk and answer the questions.

1. How many times had the man had the noodle?
   (A) 10 times
   (B) 15 times
   (C) 30 times
   (D) 50 times

2. What did the man suggest they do?
   (A) Get concert tickets
   (B) Eat steak
   (C) Eat noodles
   (D) Wait in line

3. What were they supposed to eat originally?
   (A) Pork
   (B) Steak and curry and rice
   (C) Noodles
   (D) Hamburgers

Practice D

Listen to the short conversation and choose the best statement to complete the conversation.

1. (A) (B) (C)
2. (A) (B) (C)
3. (A) (B) (C)

Unit 15 | 音の有声化

Check Point

2-36

1. I'm getting better and better every day.
2. What's the matter with you? You look sweaty.
3. What if I get a love letter from Betty?
4. Let's get off at Kings Station in Seattle.
5. I got a kick out of skydiving yesterday.
6. He's not a lawyer but a doctor.
7. How about a glass of whiskey?
8. What are you thinking about?
9. I did a lot of traveling when I was in college.
10. He's been a big help. You ought to make it up to him.
11. The tennis match was put off until tomorrow.
12. Put on your coat. It's freezing outside.
13. What a small world!
14. Did you go to the movies on Sunday?
15. I'm learning how to speak German.

● アメリカ英語の特徴として，強い強勢を受けた母音と弱い強勢を受けた母音の間に挟まれた [t] は有声化する現象があります。この [t] は，舌先が歯茎を軽くたたく感じで発音されるので「たたき音」と呼ばれ，発音記号は [ɾ] です。この音は，英語の [r] と [l] の中間音である日本語のラ行音で置き換えてもかまいません。[t] の有声化は，くだけた会話では頻繁に起きますが，フォーマルな内容の会話では無声の [t] を好む人もいます。筆者は，アメリカ人の大学名誉教授と話していた時に，university を「ユニヴァーシリ」とあえて有声化した [t] を使っていました。すると，「「ユニヴァーシティ」と発音しなさい」と注意されたことがありました。

● イメージ音

1. getting：ゲリン　better：ベラ　2.　matter：マラ　sweaty：スゥエリー
3. What if：ワリフ　get a：ゲラ　letter：レラ　Betty：ベリ
4. get off：ゲロフ　Seattle：シアロ　5.　got a：ガラ　out of：アウロヴ
6. not a：ナラ　but a：バラ　7.　about a：アバラ　8.　What are you：ワルユ
9. a lot of：アララ（of [əv] の [v] の脱落）
10. ought to：アーラ　make it up：メイキラップ　11.　put off：プロフ
12. Put on：プロン　13.　What a：ワラ　14.　go to：ゴル　15.　how to：ハル

Practice A

Drill 1 Word dictation in sentences
2-37

1. Do you want me (   ) (   ) (   ) ticket for the flight?
2. Daddy, would you spread the (   ) on my toast?
3. Mr. (   ), please don't (   ) (   ) on our conversation.
4. We should try hard to (   ) (   ) (   ) the red.
5. I (   ) (   ) (   ) for (   ) (   ) week,
   (   ) (   ) couldn't come up with a (   ) idea.

Drill2 Word dictation in dialogues
2-38

1. A: (   ), would you mind (   ) the vegetables?
   B: No, (   ) (   ) (   ).
2. A: You look depressed. What's the (   )?
   B: I (   ) (   ) D in Academic (   ) 200.
3. A: (   ) (   ) (   ) cup of coffee before you leave?
   B: Thanks, (   ) (   ) in a (   ) (   ) a rush.
4. A: Let's (   ) (   ) the magic bar on Saturday night.
   B: (   ) (   ) great idea!
5. A: How was your trip to Canada?
   B: We had (   ) (   ) time in (   ).

Drill 3 Sentence Dictation
2-39

1.
   _____

2.
   _____

3.
   _____

4.
   _____

5.
   _____

44

Practice   B

Listen to the statement and choose the best response.

1. (A) (B) (C)
2. (A) (B) (C)
3. (A) (B) (C)
4. (A) (B) (C)
5. (A) (B) (C)

Practice   C

Listen to the short talk and answer the questions.

1. When did the man get a chair?

    (A) Yesterday

    (B) The day before yesterday

    (C) Last week

    (D) Two weeks ago

2. How much did the man pay for the vase?

    (A) $ 2,000

    (B) $ 3,500

    (C) $ 4,000

    (D) $ 5,000

3. What can be inferred about the man?

    (A) He works for a bank.

    (B) He sells antiques.

    (C) He is an investor.

    (D) He is a jack-of-all-trades.

Practice   D

Listen to the short conversation and choose the best statement to complete the conversation.

1. (A) (B) (C)
2. (A) (B) (C)
3. (A) (B) (C)

音のルールから学ぶ大学生のリスニングドリル
―資格試験対応―

| 検印
省略 | © 2020年1月31日　　初 版 発 行
2022年1月31日　　第 2 刷発行 |

編著者　　　　　　　　　　　　　　　船田秀佳

発行者　　　　　　　　　　　　　　　原　　雅久

発行所　　　　　　　　　　　　株式会社　朝日出版社

101-0065 東京都千代田区西神田3-3-5
電話（03）3239-0271
Fax（03）3239-0479
E-mail text-e@asahipress.com
URL http://text.asahipress.com/english
振替口座　00140-2-46008
組版：明昌堂／製版：錦明印刷

ISBN978-4-255-15652-1

就活・留学準備の強力な味方!

あなたのグローバル英語力を測定

新時代のオンラインテスト

CNN GLENTS

留学・就活により役立つ新時代のオンラインテストCNN GLENTSが誕生! CNNの生きた英語を使った新しい英語力測定テストがいよいよ始まりました! 詳しくはCNN GLENTSホームページをご覧ください。

https://www.asahipress.com/special/glents

CNN GLENTSとは

GLENTSとは、**GLobal ENglish Testing System**という名の通り、世界標準の英語力を測るシステムです。リアルな英語を聞き取るリスニングセクション、海外の話題を読み取るリーディングセクション、異文化を理解するのに必要な知識を問う国際教養セクションから構成される、世界に通じる「ホンモノ」の英語力を測定するためのテストです。

CNN GLENTSの特長

■作られた英語ではなく生の英語ニュースが素材
リスニング問題、リーディング問題、いずれも世界最大のニュース専門放送局CNNの英語ニュースから出題。実際のニュース映像を使った「動画視聴問題」も導入しています。

■場所を選ばず受験できるオンライン方式
コンピューターやスマートフォン、タブレットなどの端末とインターネット接続があれば、好きな場所で受けられます。

■自動採点で結果をすぐに表示 国際指標CEFRにも対応
テスト終了後、自動採点ですぐに結果がわかります。国際的な評価基準であるCEFRとの対照レベルやTOEIC® Listening & Reading Testの予測スコアも表示されます。

■コミュニケーションに必要な社会・文化知識にも配慮
独自のセクションとして設けた「国際教養セクション」では、

世界で活躍する人材に求められる異文化理解力を測ります。

■試験時間は約70分、受験料は¥3,960円(税込)です。

※画像はイメージです。

お問い合わせ先　株式会社 朝日出版社　「CNN GLENTS」事務局
フリーダイヤル: **0120-181-202**　E-MAIL: **glents_support@asahipress.com**
(平日午前10時〜午後6時)